This Walker book belongs to...

NORWAY
SWEDEN
Your dad's gone raiding again!
He's gone a Viking!
SCOTS AND PICTS
NORTHUMBRIA
NORTH SEA
DENMARK
IRELAND
WALES
MERCIA
EAST ANGLIA
ESSEX
KENT
WESSEX
SUSSEX
GERMANY
ENGLISH CHANNEL
NORMANDY
FRANCE
VIKING
ANGLE
SAXON

Dear Reader,

Once there were no kings or queens. Two thousand years ago, England was split into tribes ruled by chiefs. Then the Romans conquered England and Wales, and the Roman emperors took charge. Eventually, the Romans left, partly because they got fed up defending the country from invading Angles and Saxons.

These invaders – known as Anglo-Saxons – were joined by Viking raiders, and they all fought each other to control the country. England was split into the regions of Northumbria, Mercia, East Anglia, Wessex, Essex, Kent and Sussex, each ruled by powerful leaders who called themselves kings.

Many battles were fought to bring all the regions under the rule of one king, the first king of all England. Since then, kings and queens have reigned over England, passing the role on to family or seizing power in battle! Eventually, Wales, Scotland and Ireland also came under the monarch's rule, and the United Kingdom of Great Britain and Ireland was created.

But that's jumping ahead! Let's start with the king who had the bright idea of a king of all England – and then meet every one of the 59 kings and queens that followed after him!

Be careful as you turn the pages, for monarchs can be unpredictable. Some are peaceful and kind, but others will have your head off before you can say "Your Royal Highness"!

Safe reading!

Marcia

(Happy to be a commoner and still have her head!)

P.S. That's Caw – he says he's a Royal Raven, but I think he's a pest. I keep trying to shoo him away, but he just keeps flapping back!

First published 2023 by Walker Books Ltd
87 Vauxhall Walk, London SE11 5HJ

This edition published 2024

2 4 6 8 10 9 7 5 3 1

This book has been typeset in Tryst

Printed in China

British Library Cataloguing in Publication Data: a catalogue record for this book is available from the British Library

ISBN 978-1-5295-1709-5

www.walker.co.uk

WALKER BOOKS
AND SUBSIDIARIES
LONDON • BOSTON • SYDNEY • AUCKLAND

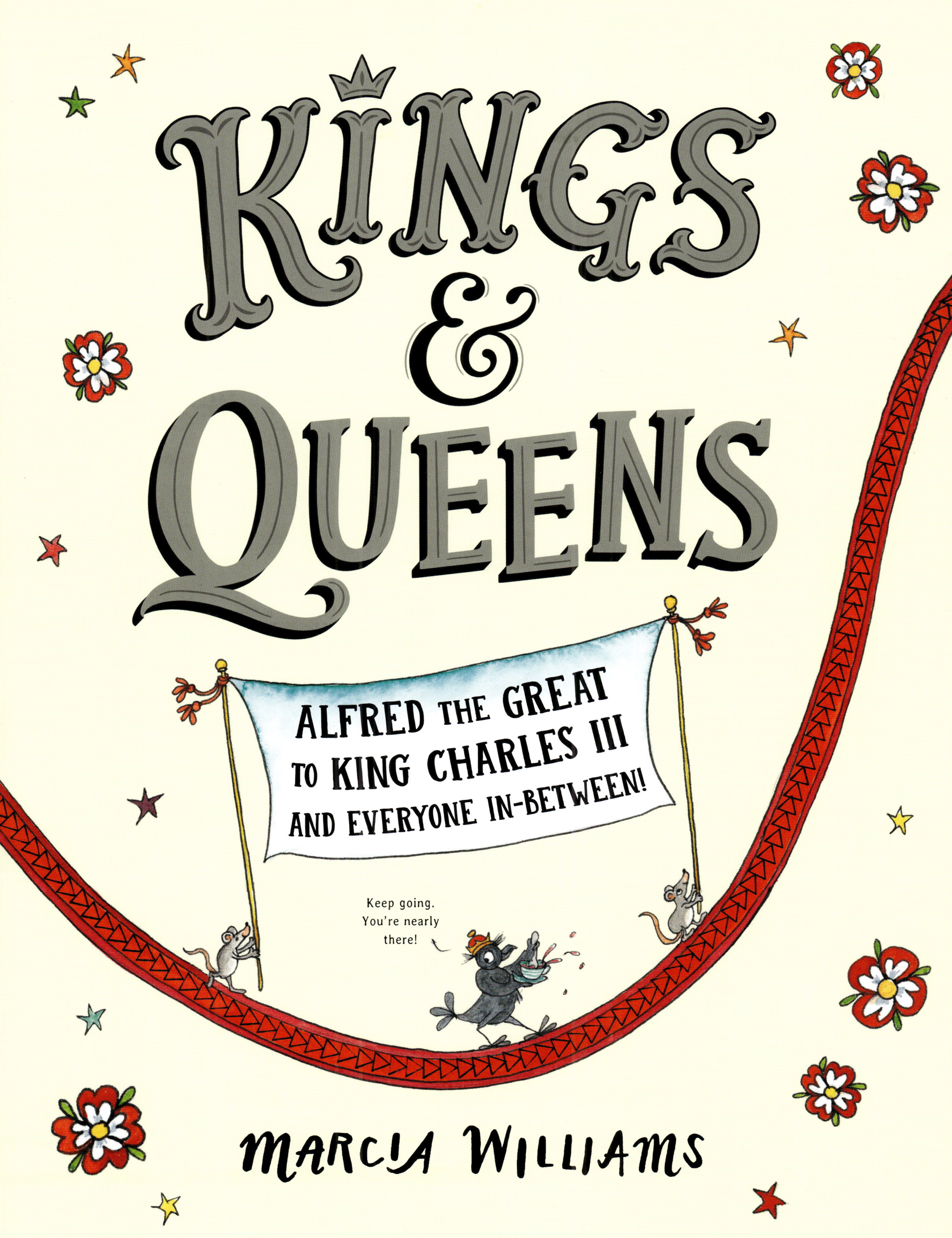

KINGS & QUEENS
ALFRED THE GREAT
TO KING CHARLES III
AND EVERYONE IN-BETWEEN!
Keep going.
You're nearly
there!
MARCIA WILLIAMS

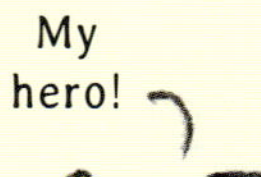

It was usual for the eldest son to inherit his father's crown.

ALFRED THE GREAT

OF WESSEX

Ruled 871–99

1

As a young Saxon boy, Alfred studied hard but was often sickly. He was the youngest son of King Aethelwulf of Wessex.

After his brothers died, he inherited his father's crown and became King Alfred of Wessex. He was keen to be a good king.

We'll stop fighting!

Maybe.

Not while we're around!

Vikings!

WESSEX

NORTHUMBERLAND

MERCIA

ANGLIA

ESSEX

KENT

SUSSEX

He turned into a formidable force and improved how his kingdom was run. More excitingly, he had an ambitious plan to make the regions of England obey one king – the king of all England!

Alfred opened schools for children.

He knew that in order to achieve this he would have to rid the land of Viking invaders.

But this was not easy, as just as one ship of Vikings fled, another one would attack!

The Vikings came from Norway, Denmark and Sweden.

Alfred signed a treaty to give the Vikings some land, earning a bit of peace. But sadly Alfred died before his dream of a united kingdom was realized. Maybe his son, Edward, would fare better?

2

EDWARD OF WESSEX

899–924

Even with the help of his fearless sister, Aethelflaed, Edward didn't quite manage to drive the Vikings from England.

3

AELFWEARD OF WESSEX

924

Poor Aelfweard died weeks after his father Edward, so he had no chance of becoming king of all England.

HOUSE OF WESSEX

ATHELSTAN

925–39

Monarchs use a house name instead of a surname. Athelstan's is Wessex because his father was king of Wessex.

Athelstan, King Alfred's grandson, was a clever, well-educated child. Alfred had doted on him and he had loved his grandpa. He hoped to fulfil Alfred's dream and become king of all England.

When, as a young man, Athelstan inherited the crowns of Mercia and Wessex, he passed just laws and encouraged trade and learning.

But Athelstan's greatest wish was always to drive the Vikings from the land, so he went north to conquer their remaining kingdoms.

Athelstan was a wise leader who built good relationships with the rest of Europe.

It appeared Athelstan had succeeded in becoming king of England, until the Vikings joined with the Scots and the Welsh and invaded England at Brunanburh. They seemed unbeatable. The fighting raged all day, with countless killed. Finally, Athelstan's enemies fled and Alfred's dream became a reality – England was united under King Athelstan.

He never married, so left no heir.

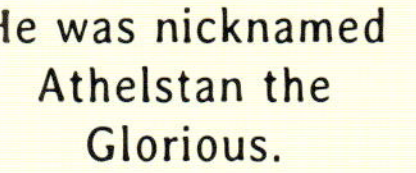

He was nicknamed Athelstan the Glorious.

EDMUND I

939–46

Edmund, known as the Magnificent, was Athelstan's half-brother and fought beside him at the Battle of Brunanburh. He was only about eighteen when he inherited the crown, but he was a good king who built on Athelstan's achievements and had peaceful relationships with allies like Scotland. It was just bad luck that he was stabbed to death by a robber he spotted in his palace.

EADWIG

955–59

Eadwig, Eadred's nephew, was only about fifteen when he was crowned and more interested in fun than duty. He made his young friends his advisers, and was accused of stealing from monasteries. He died young – nobody knows why, but it was probably just as well for England!

EADRED

946–55

Eadred, Edmund's younger brother, was a fine, religious king. But he suffered from ill health and couldn't chew his food properly. He would suck on it for a while and then spit it out! Due to his poor health, Eadred died very young and had no children to inherit his kingdom.

Zzzzz...

EDGAR

959–75

8

Edgar, Eadwig's brother, was the first king to have a large coronation. His wife, Elfrida, was also crowned. He was known as Edgar the Peaceful because he kept the Vikings away, he kept the church happy, and all of England accepted him as their king.

EDWARD THE MARTYR

975–78

9

Edward was king by the age of twelve, and dead aged fifteen. He was possibly murdered by his stepmother, Elfrida, who wanted her son, Ethelred, to be king.

After his death, Edward was made a saint.

Ethelred doesn't deserve a crown!

10

ETHELRED THE UNREADY

978–1013 and 1014–16

Ethelred was cruel and unwise. He murdered peaceful Viking farmers and gave Viking invaders money to go away, so they kept coming back for more! In 1013, he ran away to Normandy – he died shortly after returning.

When Ethelred fled, many accepted the Viking Sweyn Forkbeard as England's king.

Edmund was called Ironside because he was tough – but maybe not tough enough!

EDMUND IRONSIDE

1016

Ethelred's son, Edmund, was crowned, but many supported the Viking, Canute, for king. They fought some feisty battles, and Edmund was finally forced to share the crown with Canute. A month later, he died!

11

And that wasn't the end of the Vikings!

Canute was king of England, Norway and Denmark!
THE ANGLO-SAXONS AND THE DANES
CANUTE
1016–35
Grrr!
Canute, the Viking, was once wild and bloodthirsty.
Don't worry, I'm a new man!
Run!
But as king of England he became regal and wise!
One new monastery? Why not have three?
He built monasteries and kept the country rich and peaceful.
Canute's father was the fearsome Sweyn Forkbeard!
So great!
So perfect!
So wise!
So great!
So boring!
So perfect!
So wise!
Canute won over the English. His people worshipped him and thought his powers limitless.
12
You see, the sea doesn't listen to me.
Maybe try shouting a bit louder!
Canute found the praise tiresome, so placed his throne on the beach and told the tide to halt and not wet his feet. But the tide kept coming and his royal feet got wet. He told his adoring fans that this proved even their king had limited powers. However, he still had a popular reign!
13
He cared not for ravens, just for himself.
Harold had a reputation for rudeness.
HAROLD I
1035–40
Canute's son, Hardicanute, should have been the next king, but he was busy being king in Denmark. So his stepbrother, known as Harold Harefoot because he ran so fast, crowned himself king of England instead.

HARDICANUTE

1040–42

Call yourself my brother!

When Hardicanute heard Harold had his crown, he sailed from Denmark to kill him.

But Harold was already dead, so all Hardicanute could do was fling his body into a fen!

Let us toast!

14

Two years later, Hardicanute drank a little too much at a wedding ... and died.

EDWARD THE CONFESSOR

1042–66

Can you mend my finger?

No, I've lost the royal touch.

People believed Edward had the "royal touch" and could heal the sick.

15

Edward was very religious and had a mostly peaceful reign. But he unwisely promised his crown to both his cousin, William of Normandy, and Harold Godwinson, an ambitious earl. This resulted in an historic battle!

Edward was made a saint 100 years after his death.

Harold II was the first king who was neither related to the previous king, nor a Viking invader.

And I'm the first worm to be non-edible!

16

HAROLD II

1066

BATTLE OF HASTINGS

Even my axe is exhausted!

Soon after Harold had grabbed the crown, the Viking Harold Hardrada invaded the north of England. King Harold fought him off, but then had to dash 250 miles south to Hastings, where William of Normandy had landed to claim the throne. Harold's soldiers were exhausted, but fought bravely all day until Harold was killed. William and the Normans claimed the victory and the crown!

The Normans were Vikings who had settled in northern France.

HOUSE OF NORMANDY

WILLIAM THE CONQUEROR

1066–87

The Normans loved building castles – great for nesting!

William of Normandy gave himself a grand coronation.

He murdered anyone who didn't accept his rule.

He stole land and gave it to his Norman buddies.

William ordered a survey of land and landowners, known as the Domesday Book, to help him raise taxes.

17

William was terrifying, unjust, uncaring – and unloved!

Thousands died of poverty and starvation under his rule.

William returned to France to protect his land in Normandy.

When William died, England did not go into mourning.

Unfortunately for William, while his soldiers burned and pillaged French homes, his horse stumbled and he was mortally injured. The wound caused an infection which killed him weeks later. When he came to be buried in France, his coffin was too small and his body exploded!

William introduced the feudal system: kings and nobles were at the top with all the power, and peasants were at the bottom.

Arrows are very dangerous!
WILLIAM II
1087–1100
Oops!
18
William's son, William Rufus, was even scarier than his father! He had red hair and a red-hot temper. Alas, he was shot by an arrow while out hunting. Henry, William's younger brother, was also in the forest. He dashed off to grab the throne and royal purse!
STEPHEN
1135–54
I suppose we can do a deal...
The idea of a queen wasn't very popular with the Church.
Matilda's cousin, Stephen, stole her throne, plunging England into a civil war. Matilda nearly won the crown back but lacked support. Eventually, Stephen promised Matilda that her son, Henry, would inherit his crown.
Henry is thought to have had 27 children!
19
There's little that's worse than a greedy king.
20
Apart from a greedy pigeon!
Sucker!
HENRY I
1100–35
A bigger crown!
More food!
More money!
More land!
Henry was quick-tempered, demanding, clever and very greedy.
Death is a long time coming.
He greedily seized Normandy from his brother, Robert, and then locked him up until his death.
Yum.
Then one day, Henry ate too many lampreys and died, leaving his crown to his daughter, Matilda.
Lampreys are fish with sucking mouths. They are sometimes called vampire fish! Delicious!

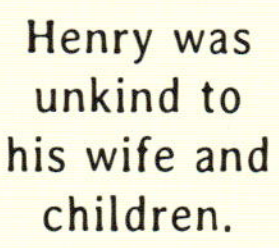

HOUSE OF PLANTAGENET

HENRY II

1154–89

Henry was unkind to his wife and children.

21

Henry controlled the nobles and introduced courts and laws that were the same for the whole country. He was clever, but had a filthy temper, which led to the death of his friend, the archbishop Thomas à Becket.

He put his wife under house arrest for years.

His sons and wife, Eleanor, tried, but failed, to dethrone him. After his son Richard led a rebellion, Henry fell ill and died. At his funeral, some people thought blood spurted from his nose, and took it as a sign he was murdered.

Richard barely spoke English.

22

RICHARD I

1189–99

The Crusades were a series of religious wars between Christians and Muslims.

Richard, known as Lionheart, spent all but six months of his reign abroad, mostly fighting in the Crusades. He cost England a fortune in ransom when he was captured in Europe, and was eventually killed in battle in France.

23

JOHN

1199–1216

Richard's brother, John, was cowardly, cruel and greedy. So to protect England, John's barons made him sign a treaty known as the Magna Carta. It gave more power to the people. John died on the toilet – possibly after eating too many peaches!

John lost the crown jewels – how clumsy!

24

Henry III, another disaster!

HENRY III

1216–72

Henry's nobles ruled for him for over ten years, as he was only nine when he was crowned. When Henry took over, disputes with barons and wars caused chaos. Some nobles and knights formed a group called parliament, who met to decide how to control the monarch!

David III, the last Welsh Prince of Wales, was executed by Edward.
Edward was nicknamed Longshanks, because of his long legs.
EDWARD I
1272–1307
25
Soon I'll make him Prince of Scotland too.
Clever and cruel, Edward improved parliament and built lots of castles. He conquered Wales and made his baby son, also Edward, Prince of Wales.
I just want to be there.
He's lost the plot, bless him!
Edward also tried to conquer Scotland, but faced fierce rebellions. Before he died from poor health, Edward asked for his bones to be carried into battle until Scotland was defeated!
Edward's second nickname was Hammer of the Scots!
Edward was a keen swimmer.
26
From 1315 to 1317 England suffered a terrible famine.
EDWARD II
1307–27
Do I deserve this?
Yes!
Edward II preferred his friends to England or his family. His wife, Queen Isabella of France, led a revolt, forcing him to give up his throne. He was imprisoned, then killed.
It's thought that Richard invented the handkerchief. Useless if you haven't got a nose!
RICHARD II
1377–99
I was a king once. Now I'm just a bundle of bones!
Edward III's grandson, Richard, was ten when he was crowned. He was a poor leader. His cousin Henry eventually imprisoned him and he starved to death.
28
EDWARD III
1327–77
27
I'm a bit of a royal whizz!
This Edward was a gifted leader, loved by his people. But when he tried to claim the French throne, he started the Hundred Years' War.
Between 1348 and 1350 millions died of the plague known as the Black Death, spread by rat fleas.
Edward III wanted a court like the legendary King Arthur, so he created a group of honourable knights called the Order of the Garter.

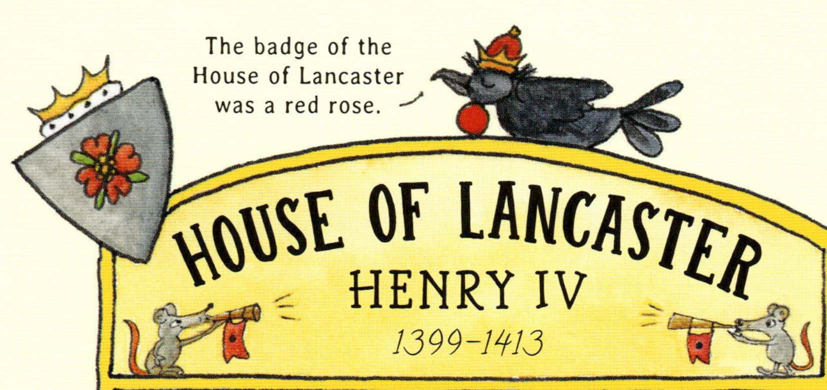

The badge of the House of Lancaster was a red rose.

HOUSE OF LANCASTER

HENRY IV

1399–1413

When Henry was crowned, his head was crawling with lice – they were delicious!

29

Henry was polite and well educated, but his reign was plagued with revolts. Many thought he had no right to be king, since he had taken the crown from his cousin, Richard. In 1405, he became ill, and his son took more control of the kingdom until Henry eventually died.

The English longbow was faster than the French crossbow!

HENRY V

1413–22

Henry was a wild teenager, but a serious and devout king. He continued the Hundred Years' War and defeated the French at the Battle of Agincourt. Sadly, he died of an infection called dysentery before he could be crowned king of France.

30

Alert: the royal nappy needs changing!

Joan of Arc was accused of being a witch and was burned at the stake.

31

HENRY VI

1422–61

Henry VI was only nine months old when he became king – even my crown hardly fit him!

Henry was a baby when his father died. He grew up to be a religious and kind king, but his reign was not great.

He hated war. He lost his lands in France thanks to the campaigns of the young French girl called Joan of Arc.

I'll have that crown, thanks.

Then Edward of York tried to steal his crown, in the wars between the Houses of Lancaster and York known as the Wars of the Roses.

The badge of the House of York was a white rose.
HOUSE OF YORK
EDWARD IV
1461–70
Run, the Lancastrians are coming!
Edward was the tallest king ever to reign, but not the bravest. When Henry VI's wife and other Lancaster supporters raised a fighting force, Edward fled the country, and Henry took back the throne – for a while, at least!
Imagine, Ed V never even got to wear his crown!
EDWARD V
1483
It's a bit big for you, dear boy.
Sadly, Edward IV died unexpectedly. His son became Edward V, but he was only twelve and his uncle and guardian, Richard of Gloucester, quickly stole the crown and made himself king.
People once said Richard was a hunchback – but it wasn't true!
32
33
HENRY VI
1470–71
AGAIN!
In 1473, William Caxton printed the first book in English.
34
EDWARD IV
1471–83
AGAIN!
35
The crown keeps swapping back and forth – I can't keep up!
36
RICHARD III
1483–85
Clever me!
I'm scared.
Me too.
Richard imprisoned Edward V and his brother in the Tower of London and in all likelihood murdered them. This was not good for his popularity!
Your crown is a perfect fit!
In 1485, Henry Tudor fought Richard for the throne at the Battle of Bosworth Field. Richard was killed and Henry Tudor crowned himself king!
This brought an end to the Wars of the Roses, hooray!

HOUSE OF TUDOR

HENRY VII

1485–1509

FACTS ABOUT ME!

I cleverly united the Houses of York and Lancaster by marrying Elizabeth of York.

I am the first king to have personal bodyguards: the Yeomen of the Guard. You might know them as Beefeaters.

I banned private armies, and without them all those nobles lost their power!

I believe in encouraging the arts and support the printer William Caxton.

I am exceptionally good at making money and brought wealth to England.

I prefer talking to fighting, so England is enjoying a period of peace.

I have a pet monkey and a lion!

I like presents: land, money and castles all welcome!

My eldest son, Arthur, died, leaving his younger brother, Henry, as my heir.

Henry just likes playing sport. I don't think he'll make a very good king!

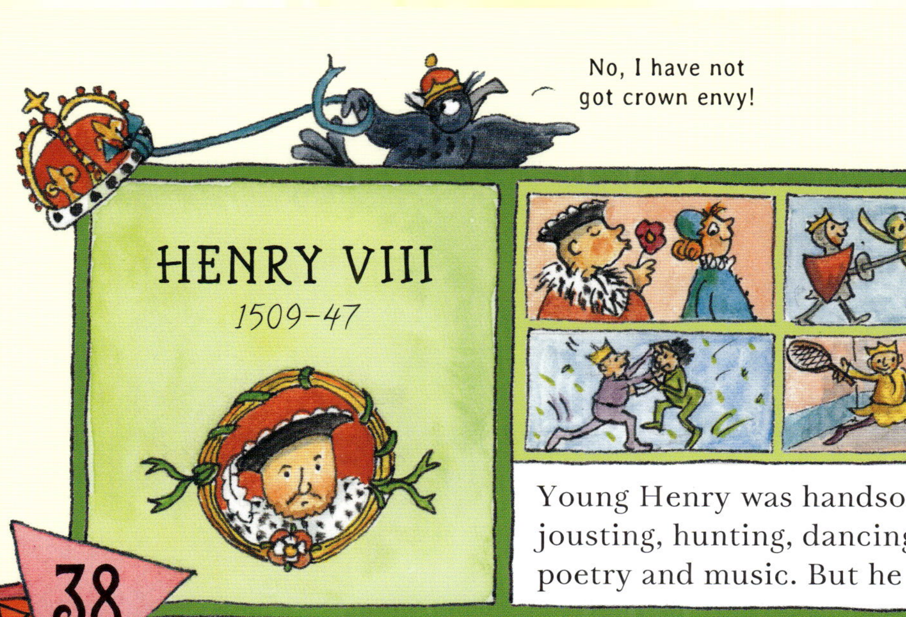

HENRY VIII

1509–47

38

Young Henry was handsome, clever and athletic. He loved flirting, jousting, hunting, dancing, wrestling, playing tennis and writing poetry and music. But he was also moody and had a filthy temper.

When Henry left the Catholic Church, he began years of religious conflict.

CATHERINE OF ARAGON

ANNE BOLEYN

JANE SEYMOUR

ANNE OF CLEVES

CATHERINE HOWARD

KATHERINE PARR

Henry could be very scary and he beheaded many people – including two of his six wives!

Henry closed the Catholic monasteries.

He was Catholic, until this meant he couldn't get divorced.

So he made himself head of the new Church of England.

Henry was an impatient father to Mary, Elizabeth and Edward.

Many members of the Catholic Church became Protestants instead.

Henry hated vegetables, but ate vast amounts of meat. Eventually, he became so overweight and unwell he had to be carried in a special chair. He died aged 55, constipated, breathless, grouchy, gouty and smelly. A sad end for the king who was once a young, active prince!

39

EDWARD VI

1547–53

A faithful Protestant, Edward was king aged nine, dead from illness aged fifteen.

Poor boy. He ordered that the crown go to his cousin next.

40

LADY JANE GREY

1553

Crowned because she was Protestant – gone in nine days!

Mary executed Jane and hundreds of other Protestants.

41

MARY I

1553–58

Mary was a Catholic; she overthrew Jane, took the throne and ruled brutally!

When Mary died, many people danced with joy!

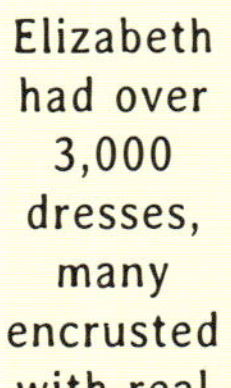

Elizabeth had over 3,000 dresses, many encrusted with real jewels.

ELIZABETH I

1558–1603

Elizabeth was the youngest daughter of Henry VIII. She was a Protestant and survived many assassination attempts by Catholics who wanted her Catholic cousin, Mary Queen of Scots, on the throne.

The Catholic King Philip II of Spain even sent an armada (fleet) of ships to invade England. But the English navy and stormy seas defeated the Spanish and not one invader succeeded in landing.

Mr William Shakespeare was born in 1564 – the queen loved his plays!

Elizabeth was very vain. She wore a wig, and put white powder on her face because her skin had been scarred by smallpox.

Elizabeth was clever, but quick-tempered. As well as executing people, she would slap, spit and throw things at anyone who displeased her.

42

In spite of her moods, Elizabeth was popular and during her rule literature, trade and exploration all thrived. She eventually fell ill and died aged 69, but not before proving that women could rule just as well as men, if not better. Elizabeth's reign – the Elizabethan era – lasted for 45 years!

Good Queen Bess had a soft spot for adventurers like Francis Drake and Walter Raleigh, as well as ravens!

Elizabeth's godson invented the flushing toilet, bless him!

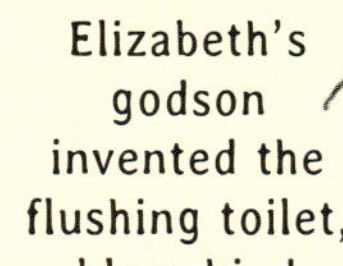
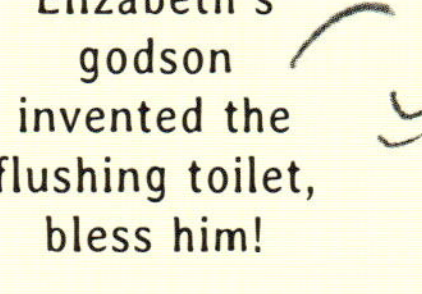

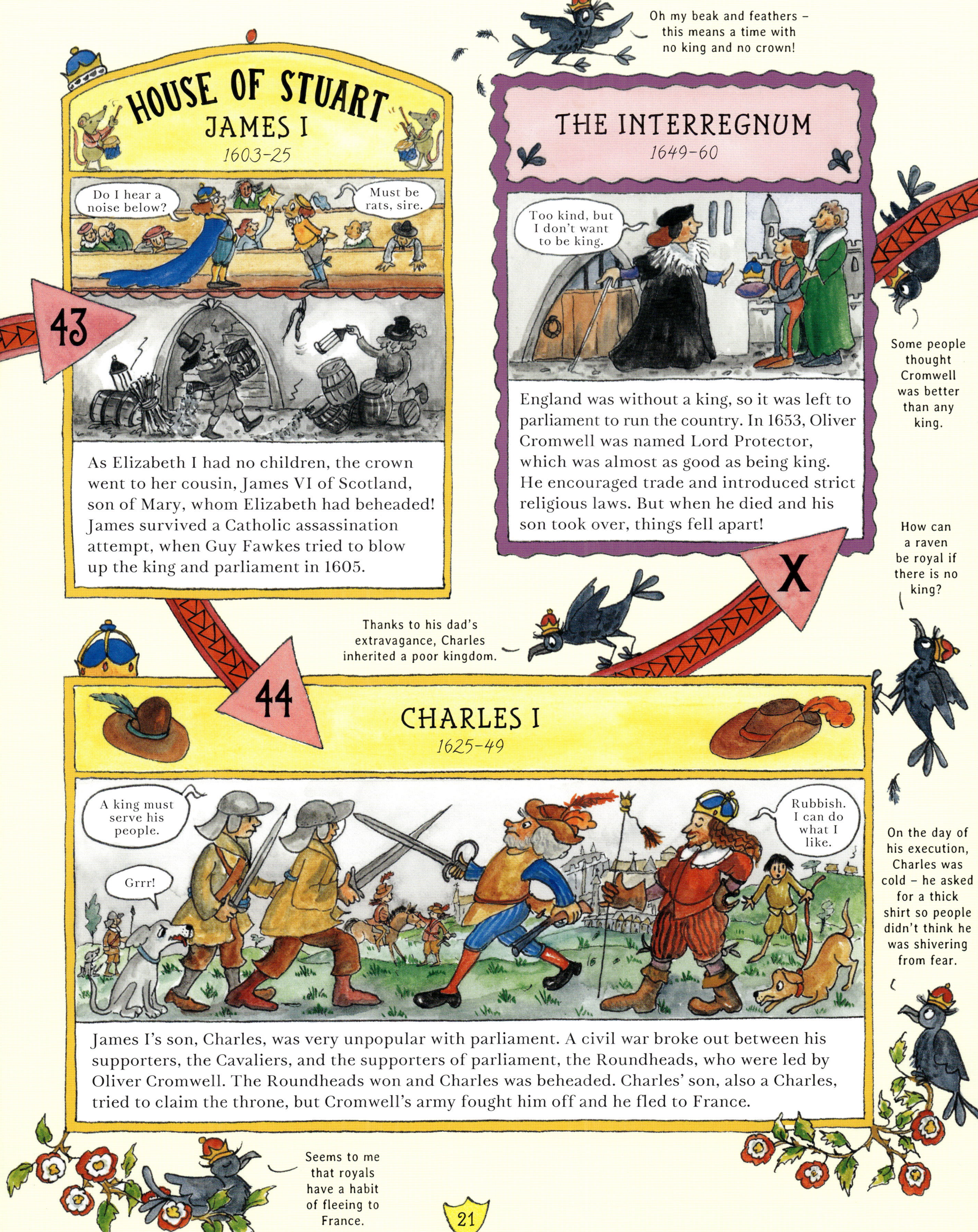

HOUSE OF STUART

JAMES I

1603–25

As Elizabeth I had no children, the crown went to her cousin, James VI of Scotland, son of Mary, whom Elizabeth had beheaded! James survived a Catholic assassination attempt, when Guy Fawkes tried to blow up the king and parliament in 1605.

THE INTERREGNUM

1649–60

England was without a king, so it was left to parliament to run the country. In 1653, Oliver Cromwell was named Lord Protector, which was almost as good as being king. He encouraged trade and introduced strict religious laws. But when he died and his son took over, things fell apart!

CHARLES I

1625–49

James I's son, Charles, was very unpopular with parliament. A civil war broke out between his supporters, the Cavaliers, and the supporters of parliament, the Roundheads, who were led by Oliver Cromwell. The Roundheads won and Charles was beheaded. Charles' son, also a Charles, tried to claim the throne, but Cromwell's army fought him off and he fled to France.

Charles was known as the Merry Monarch.
The army and navy abandoned James II!
45
CHARLES II
1660–85
Cromwell's son failed, so Charles I's son returned from Europe. He was clever and very popular.
Help! It's the plague rats again!
Plague and the Great Fire of London – what a reign!
46
JAMES II
1685–88
Charles had no heir, so his Catholic brother, James, was crowned. Parliament hated him and invited his Protestant daughter, Mary, and her husband, William, ruler of Holland, to take over. They arrived with an army and King James fled to France!
No need to behead me, I'm going!
William and Mary never wanted to marry, but ended up adoring each other.
47
WILLIAM III AND MARY II
1689–1702
Mary and William shared the crown as Mary didn't want to rule alone. They were a striking couple as she was very big and he was very small. Mary died of smallpox in 1694. William was devastated but stayed as king, until one day he fell off his horse, was badly hurt and died.
Did you speak, dearest?
It's no fun being king without you.
DO NOT DISTURB
Anne was nicknamed Brandy Nan because she liked the drink!
48
ANNE
1702–14
You're a motley lot, but you do me proud.
Attention!
When William died, Mary's sister Anne became queen. Anne wasn't really interested in ruling, but her army won lots of battles and she became popular.
People were starting to realize that monarchs were human, not godlike creatures!
United at last.
Faster!
We need help!
Anne became the first monarch of Great Britain, when Scotland joined the kingdom. In her later years, Anne was ill and had to use a wheelchair, or be carried in a sedan chair or horse-drawn chariot. Her coffin was so big it took fourteen men to carry it! With no heir, the crown went to her second cousin.
Poor Anne had eighteen children but none survived beyond the age of eleven.

George could barely speak English. He was fluent in German and French.

HOUSE OF HANOVER

GEORGE I

1714–27

George divorced and imprisoned his first wife, Sophia, for over 30 years.

49

George, ruler of Hanover, was at least fiftieth in line to the throne. But he was a Protestant and parliament had passed a law that a Catholic couldn't wear the British crown. George spent most of his time in Germany, leaving the running of the country to his first minister, Robert Walpole – Britain's first prime minister. Parliament started to run the country without real interference from the unpopular king. George died of a stroke, possibly caused by eating too many strawberries.

George II was the last British monarch born outside Britain.

George III had fifteen children. A raven could have that many in a year!

50

GEORGE II

1727–60

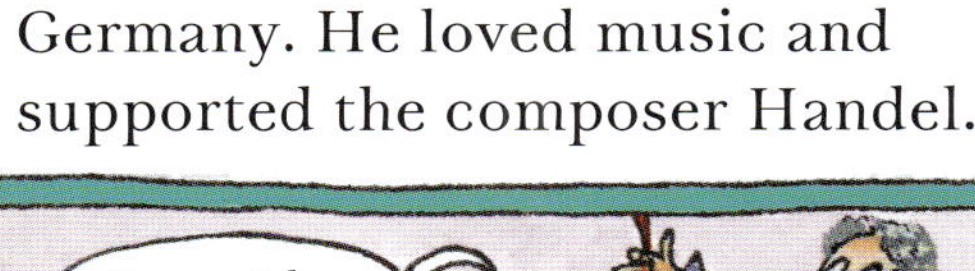

George II also preferred to be in Germany. He loved music and supported the composer Handel.

He died on the lavatory after drinking hot chocolate.

GEORGE III

1760–1820

51

George III was George II's grandson. He loved his country and his family. Britain lost its American colonies during his reign, but he was still very popular and worked hard, until he became ill.

In 1789, George Washington became America's first president: a king without a crown!

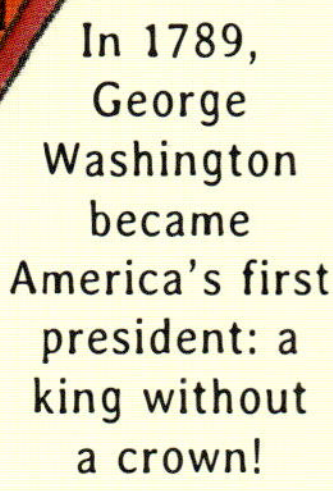

George II was buried beside his wife, Caroline. The coffin sides were removed so they could be together.

George III was nicknamed Farmer George because he was fascinated by agriculture and gardening.

This rhyme is probably about King George IV:
"Georgie Porgie, pudding and pie, Kissed the girls and made them cry..."
Daddy!
GEORGE IV
Regent 1811–20, King 1820–30
I'm such a handsome fellow!
At first, George ruled for his ill father as Prince Regent. He was vain, selfish and loved gambling. He partied and ran up massive debts.
But she has smelly knickers!
So does he!
Before George was allowed to take the throne, parliament made him divorce his Catholic wife and marry his Protestant cousin!
George could not have become king if he remained married to a Catholic.
Go away! I'm busy eating and designing a fancy new palace.
They're urgent, Majesty.
He was more interested in food and drink and building palaces than ruling the country.
You weigh twenty stone.
Who cares?
Eventually, George became so overweight and ill he hardly bothered to get out of bed!
52
William's nickname was Silly Billy!
53
George developed Buckingham Palace into the grand building we know today.
WILLIAM IV
1830–37
William was also king of Hanover, but he never visited Hanover during his reign.
Hard to starboard, crown ahoy!
George's brother William became king next. He was 64 and had been a sailor in the navy before he was a king.
They call me Silly Billy.
Kiss the king!
He wore wellington boots, and sometimes walked around London without any guards, meeting the public.
Kings and queens no longer have all the power.
Land ahoy!
William helped parliament pass a law that made them more powerful and allowed more people to vote.
Before he became king, William and his actress girlfriend had ten children!

As William's daughters both died, Victoria became his heir.

VICTORIA

1837–1901

On William IV's death, his eighteen-year-old niece Victoria became queen. She also ruled Britain's empire of countries across the world.

Luckily, Victoria had a huge personality and was ready for the challenge. She wasn't huge herself, at less than a metre and a half tall.

Her first name was actually Alexandrina.

I do, I do, I do!

I do, I do, I do!

She married her German cousin, Prince Albert, whom she adored. They had nine children.

When Albert died, Victoria dressed in black and refused to be in public for over ten years!

The Victorian age was one of invention: photography, electric light ...

The monarchy became unpopular, until Victoria was finally persuaded to go out again – and suddenly everyone loved her! Victoria ruled for 63 years while her empire grew, often sparking war abroad. She saw many changes during her reign, which became known as the Victorian age.

... moving pictures, telephones, radios, motor cars, bicycles, Easter eggs and more!

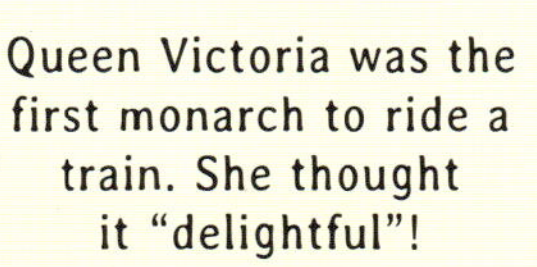

Queen Victoria was the first monarch to ride a train. She thought it "delightful"!

Edward VII's nickname was Bertie. I call him Basher Bertie.
Birds, beware: this king is a shooter!
HOUSE OF SAXE-COBURG-GOTHA
EDWARD VII
1901–10
55
I'm young at heart.
Our turn to shine.
Really?
Hello, bonjour!
What a charmer.
As a child, Edward struggled with his lessons and may have had dyslexia. In spite of this and being nearly 60 when his mother died, Edward became a fine king. He managed to continue his passion for gambling and parties, while improving Britain's reputation with visits abroad.
His shooting party once shot hundreds of birds in one day – murderer!
Between 1914 and 1918, World War I was fought between Britain and Germany and their allies.
HOUSE OF WINDSOR
GEORGE V
1910–36
Goodbye, navy.
Hello, wife and crown.
When George's elder brother died, he became heir to the throne, and had to leave behind the life he loved in the navy. He had a happy marriage to his late brother's fiancé, Princess Mary.
56
Well done, chaps!
George V didn't like parties and tried to be a good king. During World War I, he visited his troops over 450 times and was popular.
Daddy!
George changed the royal name to Windsor during the war, so that they didn't have a German-sounding name.
You wouldn't catch me giving up my crown for love!
57
EDWARD VIII
1936
VIII
Crown in one!
It's me or the crown!
Someone else can have the crown.
No!
After ruling for less than a year, George V's son Edward became the first British monarch to voluntarily give up the crown. He found royal duties boring, preferring to party and play golf. So when parliament refused to approve his marriage to the American Wallis Simpson because she had been divorced twice, Edward chose Wallis over the crown. This "abdication" made the monarchy very unpopular!
Edward and Wallis left England and went to live abroad.
Are you wondering what happens to the crown when a monarch abdicates? Well, fly over to the next page with me!

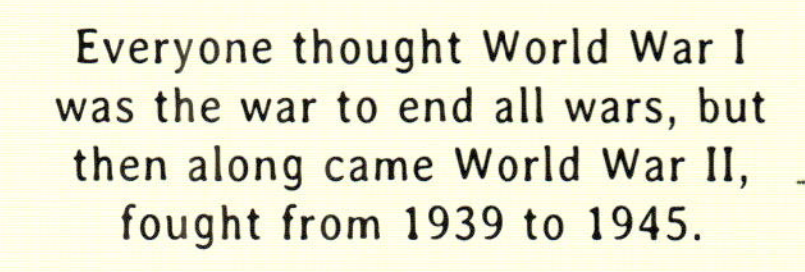

Everyone thought World War I was the war to end all wars, but then along came World War II, fought from 1939 to 1945.

GEORGE VI

1936–52

George went to a speech therapist to help control his stammer.

Edward's brother George now became king. He wasn't expecting the crown and didn't really want it.

58

He was shy and had a stammer that made speeches hard.

But he and his wife Elizabeth decided to try their best.

As did their two daughters, Elizabeth and Margaret.

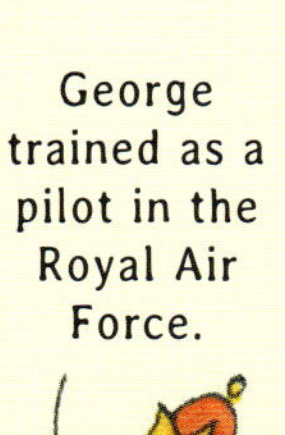

George trained as a pilot in the Royal Air Force.

During World War II they stayed at Buckingham Palace, even though it was bombed several times.

They became symbols of courage, supporting the troops and visiting bomb shelters.

He was also in the navy and fought at the Battle of Jutland during WWI.

After the war, the royal family visited South Africa, one of the countries that had become independent from Britain's empire, but which remained in a group called the Commonwealth and kept George as monarch. George's hard work and consistency made the monarchy popular again and the royal family was admired by millions across the globe. Sadly, though, George died suddenly at the age of 56.

On 8 May 1945 George broadcast a VE (Victory in Europe) Day message to his people:

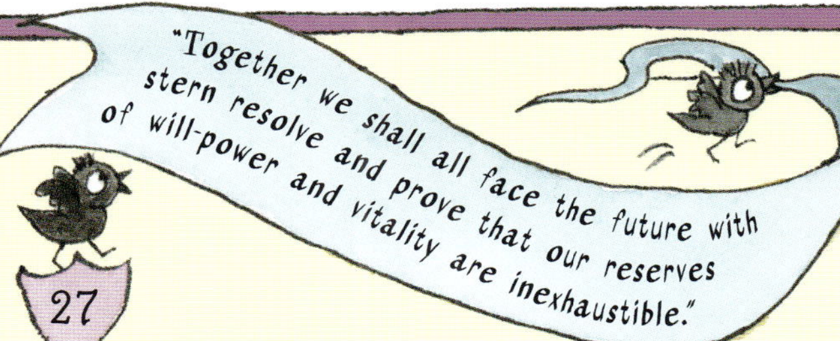

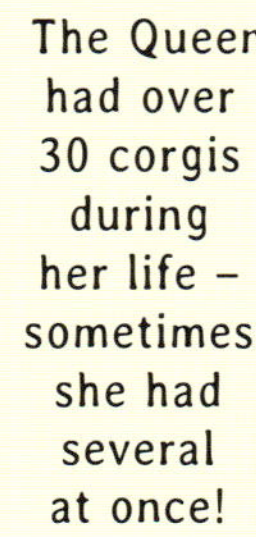

The Queen had over 30 corgis during her life – sometimes she had several at once!

Well, the Tower of London never has fewer than six Royal Ravens – so much classier than corgis!

ELIZABETH II

1952–2022

59

Elizabeth was ten when her father was crowned as king and she became his heir. Even at this early age, Elizabeth was dutiful and loyal.

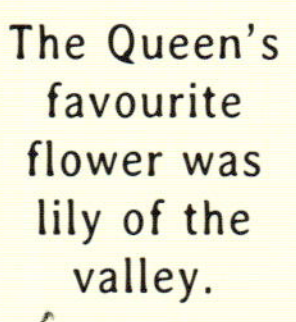

The Queen's favourite flower was lily of the valley.

During the war, she joined the Auxiliary Territorial Service.

Later, Elizabeth married Prince Philip of Greece and Denmark.

They had four children: Charles, Anne, Andrew and Edward.

She had two birthdays: her actual one and an official one.

After the death of her father, Elizabeth was crowned at Westminster Abbey. Her coronation was the first to be viewed by millions on television.

Elizabeth carried out hundreds of public duties every year, visited Commonwealth countries and entertained important guests from around the world. Just two days before she died, she appointed a new prime minister.

Queen Elizabeth II is the longest-reigning monarch in British history and gave her name to the second Elizabethan age. Although she always put duty first, she was happy when riding, watching horse-racing or walking her corgi dogs. She died peacefully at her favourite home, Balmoral, in Scotland.

The Queen once said: "Everyone is our neighbour..." Does she mean worms too?

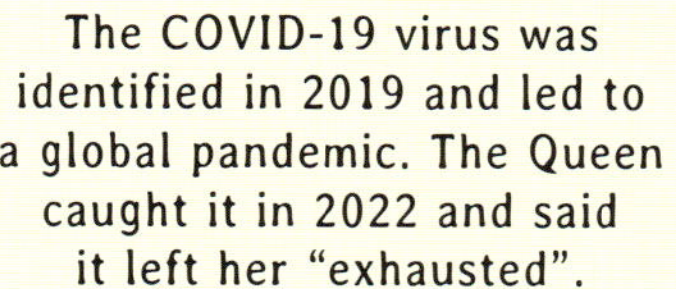

The COVID-19 virus was identified in 2019 and led to a global pandemic. The Queen caught it in 2022 and said it left her "exhausted".

Watch out Caw, Jack Russells are moving into the palace now!

Yap, yap, yap!

That's it, I'm off, and I'm taking my crown with me!

CHARLES III

2022–

Charles was 73 years old when he became king, the oldest new monarch ever. However, as Prince of Wales, Charles had taken on many duties on behalf of the Queen and supported numerous charities.

Charles' first marriage was to Lady Diana Spencer, with whom he had two children, the Princes William and Harry.

Diana died in a car accident in 1997.

He is now married to Queen Camilla, who is a great supporter of children's literacy and women's charities. King Charles is, among other things, a passionate campaigner for the environment, and has spoken up for organic farming and traditional crafts and skills.

He's not bad at laying hedges for birds to nest in!

Phew! We've made it to the end! But who's next?

The line of succession is the list of people who could inherit the crown, according to how closely they are related to the current monarch. Charles' children and grandchildren are at the top of the list.

Long live the King and all Royal Ravens!

Some people think we should have a president instead of a monarch, like in the United States. I would be a Presidential Raven instead of a Royal Raven – no way!

Yap, yap, yap!

INDEX

Aelfweard of Wessex 6
Alfred the Great 6
Anglo-Saxons and Danes 10–11
Anne 22
Athelstan 7

Canute 10
Charles I 21
Charles II 22
Charles III 29

Eadred 8
Eadwig 8
Edgar 9
Edmund I 8
Edmund Ironside 9
Edward of Wessex 6
Edward the Confessor 11
Edward the Martyr 9
Edward I 15
Edward II 15
Edward III 15
Edward IV 17
Edward V 17
Edward VI 19
Edward VII 26
Edward VIII 26
Elizabeth I 20
Elizabeth II 28
Ethelred the Unready 9

George I 23
George II 23
George III 23
George IV 24
George V 26
George VI 27

Hanover, House of 23
Hardicanute 11
Harold I 10
Harold II 11
Henry I 13
Henry II 14
Henry III 14
Henry IV 16
Henry V 16
Henry VI 16, 17
Henry VII 18
Henry VIII 19

Interregnum 21

James I 21
James II 22
John 14

Lady Jane Grey 19
Lancaster, House of 16

Mary I 19

Normandy, House of 12–13

Plantagenet, House of 14–15

Richard I 14
Richard II 15
Richard III 17

Saxe-Coburg-Gotha, House of 26
Stephen 13
Stuart, House of 21–22

Tudor, House of 18–20

Victoria 25

Wessex, House of 7–9
William II 13
William III and Mary II 22
William IV 24
William the Conqueror 12
Windsor, House of 26

York, House of 17

ICELAND
I'm lost!
SWEDEN
NORWAY
Fish for tea again?
Howl!
SCOTLAND
DENMARK
NORTHERN IRELAND
REPUBLIC OF IRELAND
ENGLAND
NORTH SEA
GERMANY
We are united!
NETHERLANDS
WALES
LONDON
BELGIUM
Land ahoy!
ENGLISH CHANNEL
FRANCE
Goodbye, ciao, au revoir! After all that history, I'm off to relax in my royal roost!

MARCIA WILLIAMS

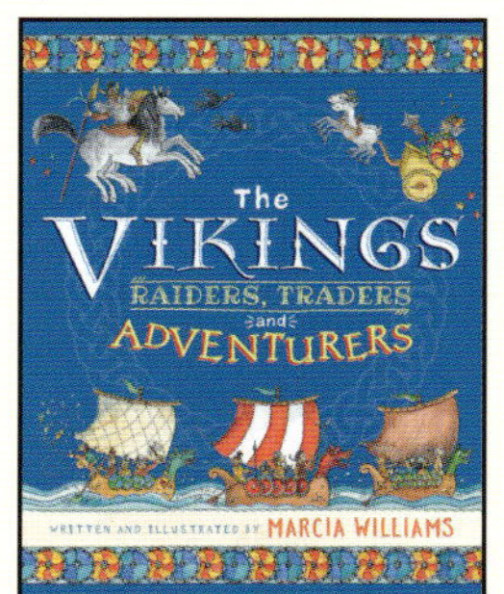

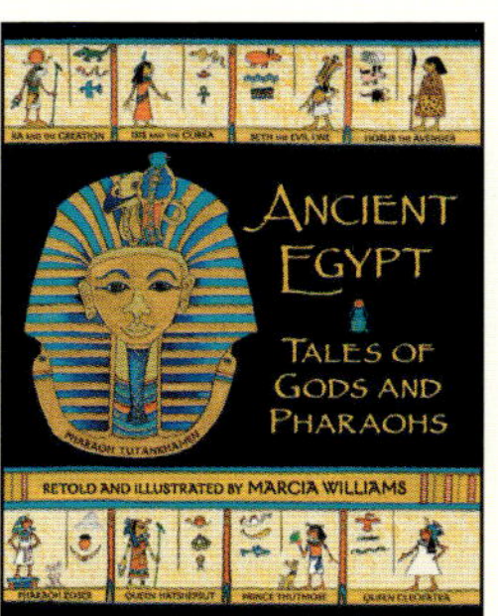

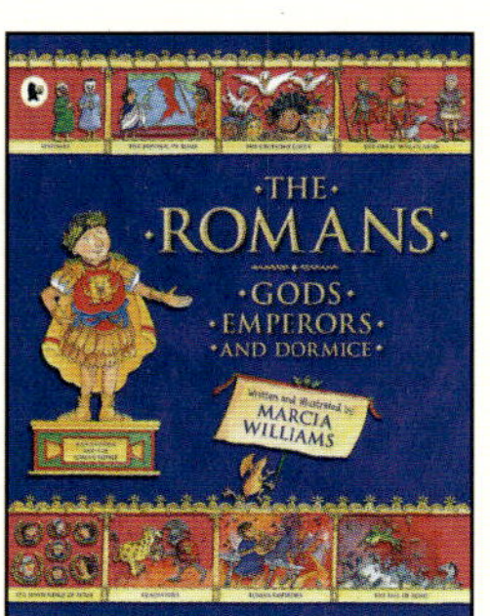

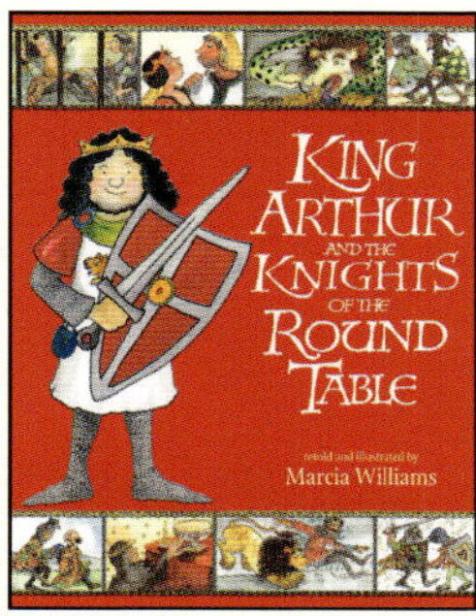

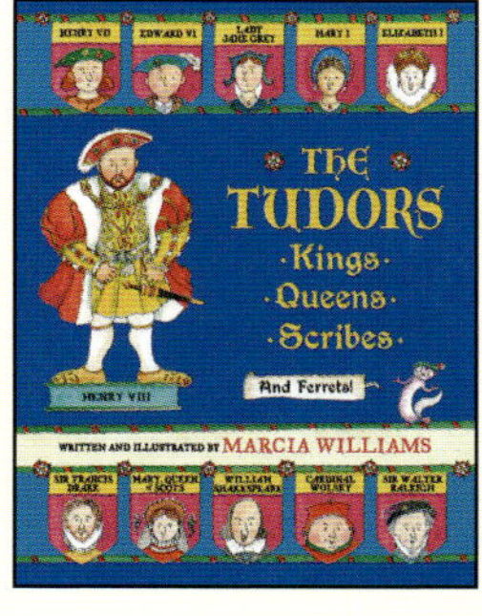

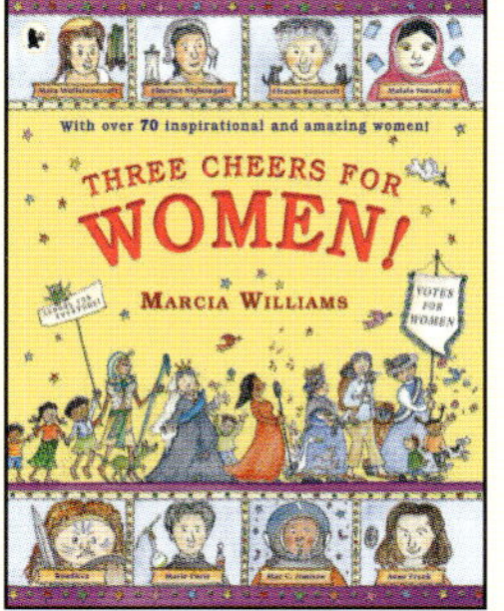

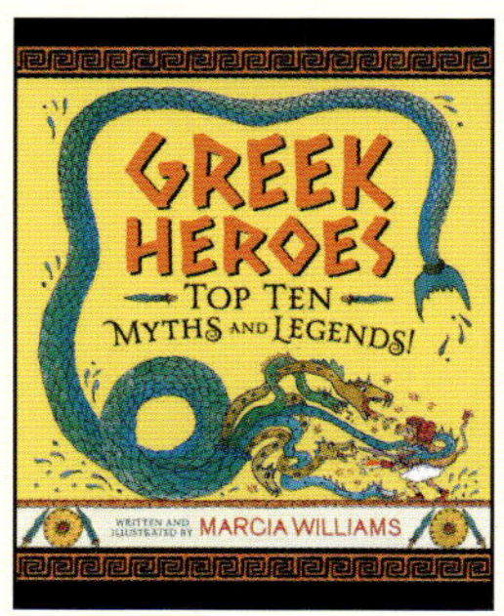

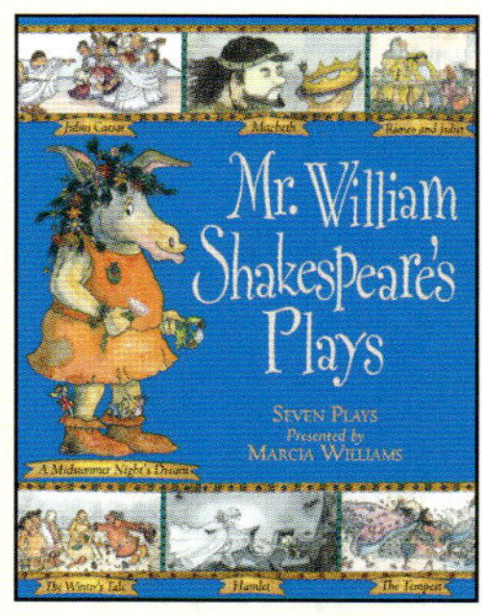

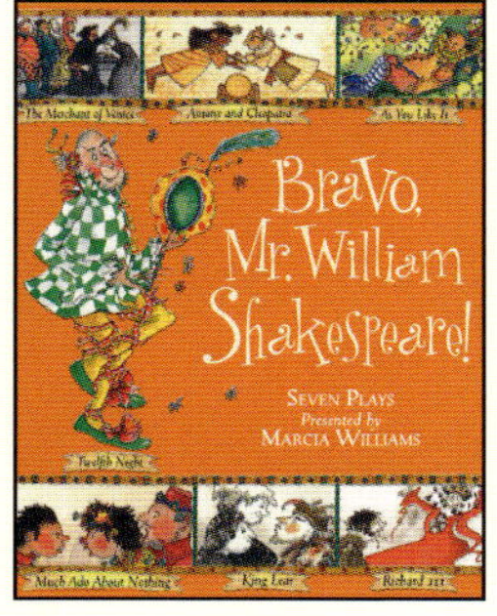

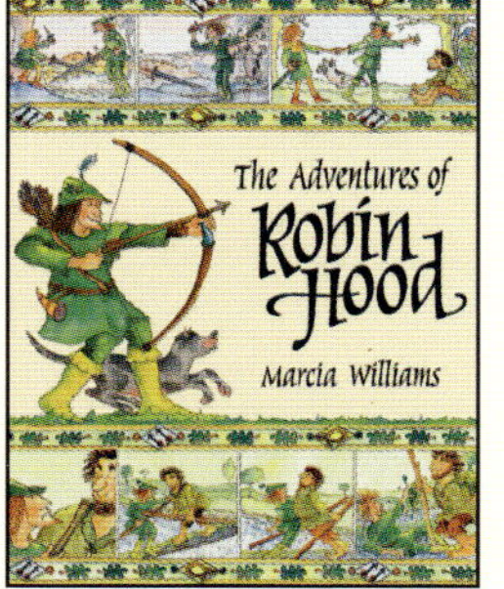

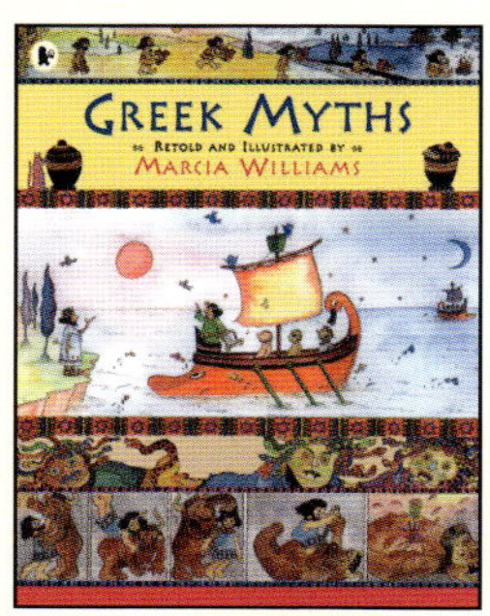

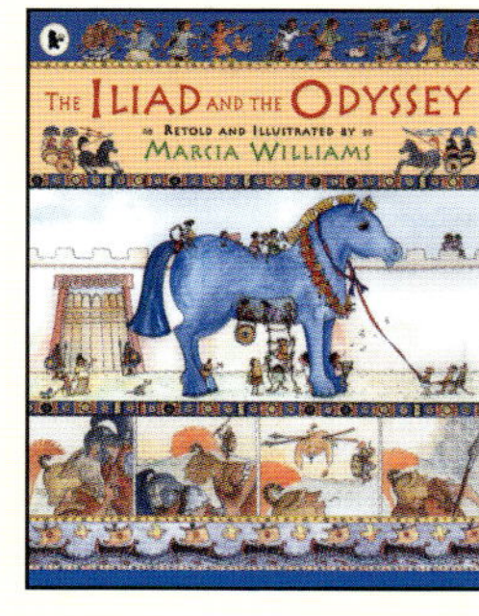

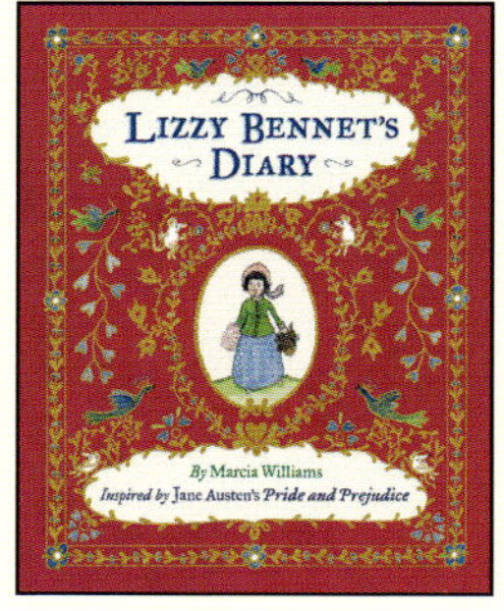

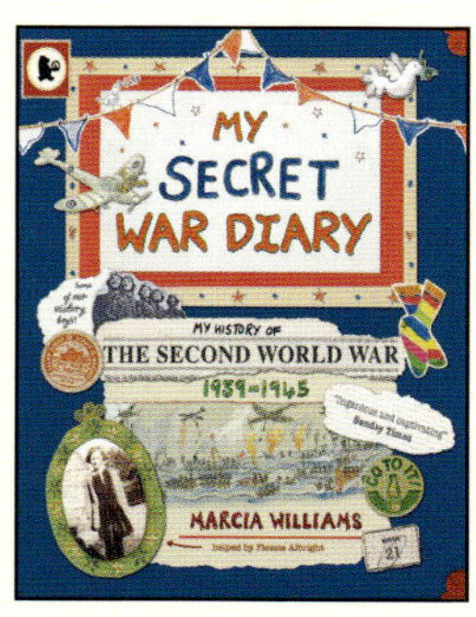

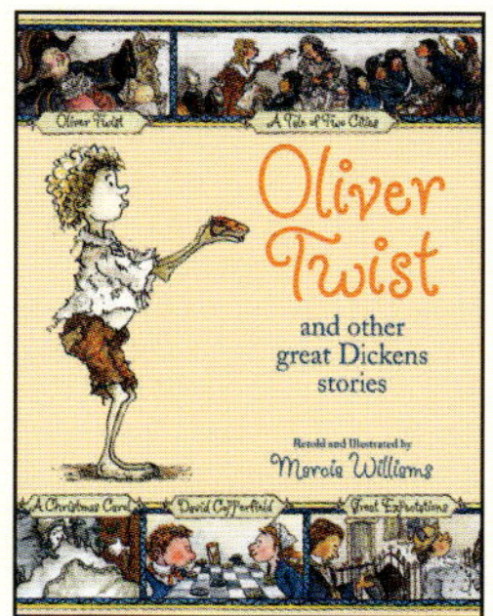

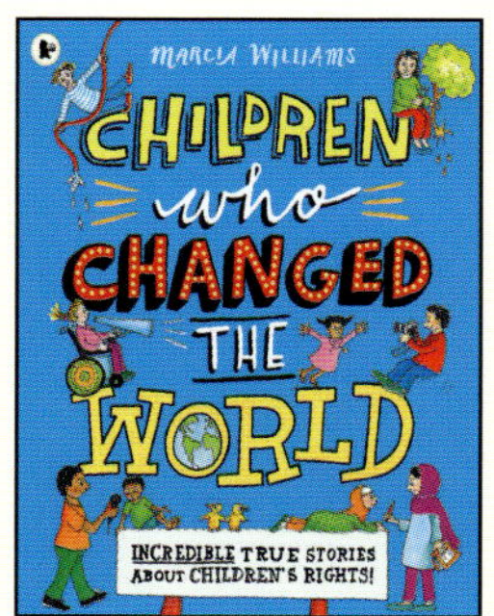

Available from all good booksellers

www.walker.co.uk